RETIRE ONCE
RETIRE WELL

"In his book, Retire Once Retire Well, Michael does a great job of coaching you through steps that will help you improve your financial life and be a good steward so you can maximize the financial blessing God has placed in your hands!

It will be a resource you'll keep coming back to in different seasons of life."

Tom Mullins
Founding Pastor, Christ Fellowship

RETIRE ONCE
RETIRE WELL

LIFE IS TOO SHORT TO RETIRE TWICE!

Michael D. Wall

"If you move with purpose,
   you will collide with destiny!"
                          -Michael Wall

About the Book

My main goal in writing *Retire Once Retire Well*, is to give clarity to its readers, helping them breakthrough the noise of our complex financial system. My desire was to put together a short, conversational, easy-to-read guide that would educate and encourage them. I want to teach them how to uncover secrets of the financial industry that are crucial to retiring well!

My wife has been a great encourager over the years, and she is continually suggesting I write things down I have not only experienced but have also been able to share professionally with families to help them make good decisions with their wealth. This became one of the main fuels behind writing this book.

You see, I view the world through the lens of a veteran financial professional, and that world is distinctly divided. Young adults tend to focus on trending market opportunities, middle-aged investors strive for the optimal balance between risk and return, and seniors shift their focus to protecting their assets and ensuring steady retirement income.

The people in each of these stages have very different perspectives and the corresponding need for a financial professional who understands their unique concerns. For the pre-retirees (executives, affluent families, entrepreneurs, professionals, small-business owners, athletes) and retirees we serve, preservation comes first. They've worked hard and saved their entire lives, and they're not interested in riding out volatile markets in the hopes that everything will work out eventually.

Many investors today are frightened and uncertain when it comes to where they should invest their money. There is so much confusion out there with endless articles and the twenty-four-hour news cycle sharing conflicting information on the different networks. At this stage of the game, investors know it's time for a different kind of planning. Over the years of helping families manage and protect their wealth, I have observed an increased desire in these people to be great stewards with what they have been blessed with.

This is why *Retire Once Retire Well* will help give investors and everyday folks, the confidence to make wise financial choices, and provide them the tools necessary to live the type of retirement they have always wanted. The idea of the title was derived from the fear and concern that investors have of outliving their savings or finding themselves in a situation where they need to go back to work to support their lifestyle. After all, NO ONE WANTS TO RETIRE TWICE!

When reading this book you will be challenged to make notes and take action as you work through the process of improving your life. This is your simple, informative guide to retirement!

Enjoy the read and I hope to see you all *Retire Once and Retire Well*! – Michael D. Wall

"To whom much is given, much is required."
-Luke 12:48

P.S. If you desire to go deeper with this process, you will want to learn more about Michael teaching the Retire Well Workbook Series for organizations and churches. Contact (888) 511-WALL (9255) or send an email to info@LeanOnTheWall.com for more information.

About the Author

Michael D. Wall is a speaker, author, coach and the founder and CEO of several companies, including Monthly Wealth Club and Wall Private Wealth. No stranger to the media circuit, Michael has appeared on CNBC, Fox Business, Bloomberg and BNN, among others. He has advised columnists for the *Wall Street Journal, USA Today, Smart Money, U.S. News and World Report, Modern Medicine, The Street, Forbes* and *CNN Money.* He has also been featured in *Forbes Magazine* under the *"Financial Leaders"* section.

Michael is the host of The Michael Wall Show, a fast-growing radio show and podcast. On the show, he shares insight on how to increase your wealth and grow your business by implementing strategies used by many successful executives and leaders who have broken through to ultimate success. Some of the guests that have joined Michael on the show have been media stars, like Sean Hannity, rock stars, like Sammy Hagar and Vince Gill, business leaders, scientists, leading health experts, professional athletes and many more. The show is heard on a variety of radio stations throughout the country and internationally through

IHeartRadio. Subscribe to the show on iTunes and other popular podcast apps. For more information about the show visit www.MichaelWallShow.com.

Michael has been a guest speaker, teaching on subjects such as protecting and growing wealth in any economy, advanced tax planning, growing a recession-proof company, and more. He also coaches and advises small businesses on how to "create a plan that works." He has spoken at several motivational events on how to live a better life while becoming more spiritually, emotionally, physically, and financially grounded. Michael has also spoken to universities and organizations such as, the University of Pittsburgh, Liberty University, Palm Beach Atlantic University, Life Action, Christ Fellowship and others.

Michael is co-author of the best-selling book *Tax Breaks of the Rich and Famous* (Millionaire Tactics That Work For Your Small Business), as well as his own best-selling first edition of *Retire Once Retire Well*.

Michael has been married to his wife, Samantha, since 2001, and together they have four beautiful children, Cyrus, Justus, Joel, and Jael. Family has been and always will be a focal point in Michael's life. He believes that raising the next generation is one of the most challenging, but truly rewarding things you could be involved in!

Michael has also played an important role in many national and local charities. He is heavily involved with Christ Fellowship, one of the fastest growing churches in the country, and serves on the board of several non-profit organizations such as March of Dimes, Life Action and SAMA.

Other non-profits he is involved with and recommends are; Place of Hope, Operation Underground Railroad, Honoring The Father, YMCA and Big Dog Ranch.

To connect with Michael Wall for advice, speaking engagements, or media interviews, please contact his team at:
(888) 511-WALL (9255)
or info@LeanOnTheWall.com.

Contents

The Reason

"There are two great days in a person's life – the day we are born and the day we discover why."
–William Barclay

I f it was easy, anyone could do it. Have you ever heard that before? I know I have. The truth is there is no real "secret" to retiring well—it really just comes down to making good choices, hiring the right help if needed, and then creating an action plan to make it all happen.

Since 2002, I have had the privilege of assisting many folks in uncovering and solving some of their greatest retirement needs and concerns. I realize that in this day and age, most folks have been turned off, or completely paralyzed by all of the so called "answers" out there today. With all of today's media outlets, it can be hard to know where to turn for the answers that are right for your situation.

This is the reason I decided to put this book together. While helping folks solve their problems in my day-to-day practice, I realized that many of their needs and concerns, as well as the discouragement they felt from previous financial help, were pretty much the same. The service they experienced was minimal, and they were tired of taking the roller coaster ride of the market. They were also looking for a more holistic approach, an approach where all of the aspects of their retirement were addressed, not just basic growth strategies. I'm talking about incredibly important aspects like Estate Planning, Tax Reduction Strategies and Long Term Care needs.

Most of the families I've assisted, were simply looking for a professional to step up to the plate and take on the role of being their personal CFO (Chief Financial Officer). So, for the purpose of this book, consider me your personal CFO! When you are done reading, if you don't head down the path to a better future, the only one you will have to blame is yourself! I realize the information you will read just scratches the surface of a full-blown plan, but the knowledge you gain will start you down the right path to success!

As you read this book, here are some questions to ask yourself. You will want the answers to ensure that your future retirement is on the right track. Remember, the more interactive you become with the process of your success, the better chance you'll have of being successful!

Key Point:

When you think of your goals, you need to be very specific. List every goal you have, and determine which ones are most important. Don't be generic.

✞ What are YOUR future goals?

Yes, I want you to take a few minutes and list your goals! Remember success requires action!

1)

2)

3)

4)

After you have set your goals, the next step is to create specific plans to help you achieve them. What processes and types of accountability have you incorporated into your life to give you the best opportunity of reaching your goals? You must ask yourself if you are open and willing to accept new ideas that might be and probably will be outside of your comfort zone!

Almost everyone wants to have a good life, a successful retirement, and the financial peace of mind necessary to be able to choose the type of lifestyle they want to live. For this reason, I fully believe in the fact that "If you do the things you need to do, when you need to do them, the day will come when you can do the things you want to do when you want to do them," a popular quote from an old buddy of mine, Zig Ziglar. So, the next question on your journey is…

✝ Why do you have your current investments?

More work, I know! Success takes time and your future is worth it!

1)

2)

3)

I realize this might sound silly, but it is important for us to drill down and find out exactly why we own what we own, or do what we do with our money. Believe it or not, buying things that you don't really need, but just WANT, will certainly hinder the process of obtaining the retirement you've always wanted. If you already have a solid plan in place that you KNOW will allow you to be where you want to be in the future, then by all means, spend away!

The reason this question is important is that, as people, we generally make better decisions about why we do what we do if there is a reason behind it. For example, maybe you are close to retirement and your portfolio looks pretty similar to how it looked 10 or 15 years ago. You have your monies allocated in ways that you were used to, and only make investments that you were comfortable with while you were in your working years. This could be a setup for significant failure!

Things are different in retirement than in your working years, and you must plan accordingly. The question that we need to prepare for is, are you ready for twenty to forty years of unemployment, otherwise known as retirement? This is a great question!

Retirement isn't often looked at in this manner, but when it is, a plan can be created to make those years truly golden.

Each investment you own must have a specific purpose. The old rule of thumb was to achieve a certain amount of wealth and then live off of 4% or 5% of those monies for the rest of your life. Many retirees have found this strategy as flat-out unworkable for them. Often, this happens because of something in retirement that you will encounter if you are taking income from your portfolio. This "something" is a big deal and it's called Reverse Dollar Cost Averaging (RDCA). I will cover this in more detail later in the book because it is a powerful, and sometimes detrimental force, which you must plan for.

You just read about the importance of your goals and the need to be specific, so I thought I would share with you my goal for you as you read this book. My hope when putting this book together was to create something brief, specific, and valuable to the reader, bringing clarity to them regardless of age. I know that if you embrace the new ideas in this book, you will have a much more successful retirement.

Why is this important to me? I believe that our nation is in a state of decline, and it is more important than ever for individuals to take personal responsibility for THEIR futures! If more people take responsibility and have great success in their retirement, I believe it will affect the nation as a whole, positively! Remember, you are the only one who will live your future, and the choices you make now will have huge impact on whether or not it is an enjoyable one.

Notes:

Hope Is NOT A Strategy

"A dream becomes a goal when action is taken toward its achievement." –Bo Bennet

It seems like in the past decade or so we have heard a lot about hope and change. Unfortunately, what we most often see is that these words are spoken, but little changes for the better in the long run. A lot of folks have tried to live on the hope that their previous financial professional gave them, but unfortunately, most of the previous planning they have utilized either doesn't fit their current stage of life or addresses only a small portion of their "big picture" needs.

WARNING: One thing you must be aware of is that a lot of so-called financial professionals are merely nothing more than asset gatherers. Think about it this way, how stable would a three-legged stool be if only one leg was attached to the seat? This is how many of these "financial professionals" go about helping folks with probably the most valuable part of their financial life, and in a lot of cases, what took them their entire lives to build.

This is why seeking out a professional who has *a true, well-rounded approach*, which includes helping you protect and grow your assets while also introducing solid tax planning and estate planning, is an essential key to a successful retirement. You have heard it said before, "You get what you pay for," and in most cases, this rings true in the financial world.

Many people live on the island, SOMEDAY ISLE. They say, "Someday I will do this, and someday I will do that," and for some reason *someday* never gets here. Maybe you have caught yourself saying this recently. I know I have observed times in my life where that was the case. This is a thought process that we MUST get away from! We need to move toward a reality where we will make decisions to improve our futures now! Benjamin Franklin once said, "You may delay, but time will NOT, and lost time is never found again!"

It is amazing to me how many folks who first come into our office, or have a consultation with us over the phone for a second opinion on managing their wealth, (or tax-planning, financial help, business coaching, or even estate planning ideas), have important issues in their life that they need to address, but for some reason keep putting it off. It is like the founder of a procrastination club saying, "I promise, we will start the club tomorrow!" Procrastination does one thing; it makes you more stagnant and comfortable with your current circumstances. If we are brutally honest, it even makes you lazy.

So how does all this relate to your financial future? Taking no action to complete necessary steps to ensure your success will absolutely bring you more fear, worry, stress, and ultimately, failure in your retirement years. You may have heard the phrase "failure is not an option," and when you start to think this way about your future and make decisions accordingly, your chances of success will dramatically increase. Even though you may have heard all of these thoughts before, I take the time to express them because I know that regardless of how great your hopes are for your future, if you don't take action, nothing will happen.

So, now that we are all motivated and committed to taking the appropriate steps to ensure a better future, let's make sure we choose strategies that allow us to get there, not just hope we can get there. What this really means is that when creating a strategy for your financial future we must understand that everything has a string attached to it. I know I let the cat out of the bag, but when we look at our options this way, I believe things make much more sense.

What does having a string attached mean? It means there are positives and negatives to everything, and you must find which equation works best for you.

For example, working out can be boring or even painful for some people, but the end result of consistent, disciplined exercise is that you will feel better, probably look better, and will have more energy and overall excitement about life.

The string in this example would be the pain or even that it can be boring, but when we take a look at the positives, we can make a strong case that these strings might just be a perfect fit for our life!

Key Point:

Our lives are made up by a series of choices. What will you choose, success or failure?

It's really all about what YOU choose to notice. If you are willing to take the time and put in the effort, you will find the right professional to help you along the way. You must be prepared, though, to be open to new ideas, even ideas that may not be popular with the mainstream media or large financial institutions, or even Wall Street. Once you get to this point, you are ready to entertain and implement REAL solutions that will take you where you want to go.

It can often be easier to blame others on what happens to you or where you end up in life, but if you take full responsibility, (that means 100%), you will find that opportunities seem to come your way! We often find what we are looking for.

Have you ever purchased something, say a white car, and all of the sudden noticed white cars are everywhere? Similarly, when you choose good choices and accept advice from the right people, you will find yourself in a place that is moving you to where you want to go!

BEWARE:

When you are ready to accept advice, there will be many unqualified people eager to give it to you! A good friend of mine, Todd Mullins, who is Lead Pastor of Christ Fellowship, always shares the importance of choosing wisely who we allow to speak into our lives. Don't let this caution keep you from getting advice, just make sure the advice your receiving is from someone who has your best interest at heart and is knowledgeable on the topic.

Steps to take NOW!

1)

2)

3)

4)

Notes:

Gain And Retain

N ow that sounds like a good idea, doesn't it? First you gain money, then you retain what you have gained! This idea might be much simpler than you think if you get the right financial help! A great way to retain what you have gained is to be sure that your investments have been set up in such a way that you fully know the risk you are taking and how much you can or cannot lose. Paying attention is the key.

At this point, we need to really understand and be OK with the stage of life that we are in. For our purposes, there are really only two stages of life. The first stage is the accumulation stage. This is the time when you are working for a company, you own your own business, or do whatever you do to generate income. With the monies that you earn, you take portions of it every year and put it away, save it, or invest it to try and plan for a comfortable retirement.

Now, in this phase we have several factors working for us that we must consider. First, we usually have time on our side. Second, we have the ability to increase our income by working harder or working smarter, which oftentimes gives us the ability to have extra money to save for the future. Another important detail about the accumulation phase is that in this phase you generally don't take monies out of your portfolio. The total focus is growth. Since we have time on our side, we also enjoy the benefits of compounding interest and the investments we utilize in this stage are typically more market driven. These investments may have a little more risk, but the reward can be much greater.

If you have never heard the story of the doubling penny, I would encourage you to google it and learn about the power of compounding and the value of time.

The next phase is the distribution phase. This is the time when you are very close to or already in retirement. In my opinion "very close to" retirement is five to ten years away from the day that you want to retire. This is the time, I believe, where you must change the way you start to look at risk versus reward, as well as making sure you are confidently putting a plan into place that will allow your future monies to be as tax efficient as possible. Remember, taxes can often be your biggest expense!

As I will discuss later in the book, our goal for the folks we work with is to help them grow their wealth safely while looking for strategies that will enable them to morally, legally, and ethically disinherit the IRS, not only in the current year, but also for years to come! This goal must become yours in order to maximize your wealth in the future.

In the distribution phase, some significant changes take place which I believe most people really don't take the time to consider. When you are retired you are usually no longer creating new workable income, which takes away the element of adding to your portfolio each year. You also have much less time on your side than you did when you were in your thirties or forties even if you do live to the ripe old age of 100! Both of these factors, together, can create a HUGE financial storm in your life, which I will cover in a later chapter of this book.

The **major point** to take from the distribution stage is that factors in your life have shifted and you must be willing to change your thinking to align yourself with the ability to have a successful distribution stage as well. When we were children we ate baby food. Now we are all grown up and would much rather have a steak, if you're a meat eater that is! Change is necessary.

I had a conversation with a client in which we talked about growing money, which was very important to him, as it should be. As we continued our discussion, I asked, "If we take your portfolio and safely double it over time and then you walk out on life (pass away) and leave all of the monies and the growth to the kids, but before it goes to the kids, 50 percent or more goes to the government in taxes, who really won?" After he thought about it for a while, the answer he came up with was the government, which is the right answer.

So, in the distribution stage, we must consider many other factors besides just what we make on our money. If we effectively adhere to investments that are right for us in this stage of life, the chances of a successful distribution stage dramatically increase! In addition, some of the nonfinancial benefits to this type of thinking in the distribution stage are increased peace of mind as well and the ability to really enjoy your retirement years.

Notes:

Notes:

Flea Training

"Thoughts, like fleas, jump from man to man, but they don't bite everybody." –Stanislaw Jerzy Lec

You have to be asking yourself, "Is he serious?" How does flea training relate in any way to the financial world? Yes, I am serious and flea training relates more to finances than you think, especially how we think about finances. So, what is it all about?

It is really simple. You may not have known this but you can actually train fleas. In fact, if you take fleas and you place them in a jar and put a lid over them, they will jump up and hit their head against the lid. OUCH! That hurts, of course, so over time the fleas will become conditioned to only jump high enough so as not to hit their heads on the lid.

Now, if you're not aware, fleas are pretty smart. It reminds me of the two fleas at the bottom of the hill. One said to the other, "Should we walk or take the dog?" Joking aside, what fleas will do after they feel the pain from hitting their heads on the lid of the jar, is continue to jump, but only high enough so that they won't hit the lid.

You are probably still saying, "How does that relate to people and finances?" I'll tell you. People also have the ability over time to be "conditioned" by pain.

Think about it, many of you reading this book probably lost money in 2001. Do you remember what happened on 9/11/2001? It was an extremely sad day for this country. Unfortunately, as a result of the terrible act that occurred, the stock market continued its dive down and almost everyone who had money tied into the markets lost a significant amount of that money. Now, I know that the markets from 2002, all the way up until about the third quarter of 2007, were pretty strong and most people made all or most of their loss back and were in the positive again. What they did not realize was that they were starting down the road of being conditioned by the markets, again.

All of the sudden in 2008, the market took another major dive and many folks again lost 30%, 40%, and even as much as 50% of their portfolios. Ouch, now that really hurts! Now, many were really starting to be conditioned to think maybe the retirement they always wanted might not be a real option.

This is a scary place to be and so many people are looking for alternate ideas to try to bring safety into their portfolio. I want to congratulate you on picking up and reading this book because it means you are still searching for solutions to help you reach your goals! The good news is that there are strategies and solutions out there in which many people in 2001, and 2008, lost little or no money at all from their portfolios. One thing to consider in retirement, or (as we mentioned earlier) the distribution phase of life, is that the less we lose, the more opportunity we have to build a real plan that will ensure our money is there for us.

In simple terms, **ZERO IS YOUR HERO.** I'm talking about zero loss, that is. If you can find strategies that will help you reach your goals without taking risk, why would you take risk? By the way, a question that I always ask folks who have lost money in the past is "How much gain did you really make in the years your portfolio was growing to get back to its original value before the loss?" The answer is pretty simple—nothing.

So, even though in the past there may have been times, and in the future there will be times when you will feel uncertain about the world around you, if you keep searching for answers, you will find them! This is why it is crucial that you find a professional who will guide you to solutions that not only make sense for your stage of life, but also help you implement strategies that are designed to significantly reduce taxation on your portfolio today and in the future.

Now do you see how flea training and the way we think about finances go hand in hand? It is important to be aware of the fact that we can be conditioned, financially. This should motivate you to take the necessary steps and get the right financial help. Remember, in your retirement the only thing I believe you should be worried about is where your next vacation is going to be and what type of life you want to live. That might mean volunteering somewhere or spending more time with the family. Whatever the goals, one thing you should not have to worry about is whether or not you can live the way you want to live and do the things you want to do. A solid plan for your future will help reduce that worry.

> "Someday you will either say, I'm
> glad I did, or I wish I had."
> -Zig Ziglar

Notes:

Notes:

Uncovering Strategies To Protect Your Wealth

"The gratification of wealth is not found in mere possession or lavish expenditure, but in its wise application." –Miguel de Cervantes

You are probably asking yourself, "What strategies can we uncover that will help me protect my wealth?" There are many forces at work on both the wealth accumulation side and on the wealth preservation and distribution side of life. I felt it necessary to uncover a factor that can absolutely destroy a portfolio in retirement, if it is not addressed.

Over the years I have found that Wall Street typically doesn't discuss things that can adversely affect your money in retirement. Why? I don't know. Many would argue that big banks and investment companies are more interested in your money staying where it is, than diversifying it in a variety of different on and off market investments. However, this diversification will not only help reduce your risk but will also help reduce the force that works against you in retirement.

That force is RDCA. RDCA simply stands for Reverse Dollar Cost Averaging. When it comes to investing while you are in your working years, you were probably familiar with dollar cost averaging (DCA). This is the idea that you invest money on some type of a regular basis, whether monthly, quarterly etc., and the purpose of doing this is to take advantage of the market as it goes up and down. As the price of whatever you invest in fluctuates, the new monies invested take advantage of higher and lower prices as the market moves, which ultimately average out your cost of the investment you own.

You can apply this idea to any type of investment: stocks, bonds, mutual funds, exchange traded funds, options, futures as well as certificates of deposit (CDs) and annuities, as interest rates themselves change. You can also apply this strategy to real estate. The price of property fluctuates as the market demand changes.

So how does RDCA differ from DCA, and who can it affect? RDCA primarily affects those who are close to or currently in retirement. Fewer and fewer people today can look forward to a pension when they retire. Many will sell their businesses, or look to roll a lump sum of money from a 401k, 403B, profit sharing, IRA or some other type of retirement account. Since this is now the account from which they will need to produce a "paycheck" in retirement, the way this money is invested becomes extremely critical. This lump sum of money is now critically important to sustaining their retirement lifestyle.

Obviously, when you are taking monies out of an investment, you are no longer putting monies in. So, the benefit of DCA goes away. At this point, RDCA comes into play. In fact, some of you may have experienced the effect of this on your own portfolio through years of heavy market downturn.

You have heard people say that the general rule of retirement was to obtain a certain investment portfolio size while you are working, and then when you retire, withdraw 5% (now changed from 2-4 %) of your portfolio, and it should last you for life. We've all heard that story before and yet many retirees are still fearful they will run out of money. Why are they fearful? It is because of RDCA.

Let me give you an example of how this can affect your future. Let's say you have $1,000,000 of liquid assets that you plan to take income from over the course of your retired life and you were planning on taking 5% a year from that $1,000,000 portfolio. Now, if the market made exactly 5% per year, every year, that would absolutely be a doable objective. Unfortunately, that is not what happens in the real world.

Based on the past 100 years or so of market movement, the market will more than likely go up and down. When it will go up and down and by how much we don't know for sure. So, getting back to our example, if you have $1,000,000 and you start taking 5% per year out as income, whether it be dividends or interest earned, you would be taking $50,000 per year in income. The problem comes in when the market has a bad year. Think back to 2008, when many folks lost 30% to 50% of their portfolio. If you were taking income from the $1,000,000 in that year and you lost, say, 30%, your portfolio value would now only be around $700,000, and that does not even include you taking out the $50,000 for income.

Reverse Dollar Cost Averaging

$1,000,000 Retirement Assets

5% a year = $50,000

Unless you lose $ in the market

$1,000,000 @ 5% = **50k**

What if we have Another 2008 and you see a -30% drop in value

New Value is $700,000 @ 5% = **35k**

Chance of outliving your money much greater

If you continue to take income the next year, you will be taking that $50,000 from a $700,000 portfolio and, by doing simple math, you know that it will take more than 5% to achieve that $50,000. Even if the market starts to come back up the heavy reduction of portfolio value in conjunction with the income taken will greatly increase the chance of you running out of money in your lifetime, unless you reduce the amount of income you take, which from my experience, has never happened.

So, how do you avoid this hazardous trap? One great way to do this is by "laddering" your money and adding investments to your portfolio that offer no market risk. When you ladder your money, you put certain amounts of money in different investments designed for a specific purpose. This has become one of the most effective ways to maximize your wealth in retirement! Make sure you seek out an independent advisor when you are looking for the right financial guidance with your wealth. When a financial advisor is independent, they can often bring a blend of unbiased strategies to the table to engineer a portfolio more suited for your needs in retirement.

It is so crucial to make sure you have a portfolio engineered just for YOU! This allows you the ability to not only reach your goals, but also ensure you never have to change your lifestyle!

Notes:

Benefits Of Tax Planning

"Thinking is one thing no one has ever been able to tax." –Charles Kettering

It amazes me that in the advanced society we live in today, with all of the products and services we have produced as a country over the years to truly benefit people, we still have a tax code from the government that is so complex that most folks have no idea where to start when it comes to understanding it! This is one of the reasons I was happy to co-author the book *Tax Breaks of the Rich and Famous*.

One of the goals we have at our firm is to look for ways to legally, morally, and ethically DISINHERIT THE IRS! Most folks that we come in contact with are familiar with tax preparation, but they are not familiar with the idea of real tax planning. My goal in this chapter is to lay out the benefits of utilizing tax planning in your financial life. Think about it, if you could keep more of your money and give less to the government, is there any reason you wouldn't do that? If you're paying attention, the answer should always be, NO!

To start, we must make a distinction between tax planning and tax preparation. Tax preparation is something everyone who reads this has probably either done personally or had done by professional, such as a CPA (certified public accountant) or tax preparer. Tax preparation is simply accounting for all of the monies you spent in a given year as well as all monies you earned in the same year. You would then determine what things you spent money on or donated to that would be allowed to be a tax deduction for the given year.

The result will let you know what you were eligible to get back on your tax return or what you owed to the government in taxes. All of this is important to know, but unfortunately a problem can arise when you do this process year over year with little to no change in your tax status. We have found that you can fall into the rut of becoming reactive instead of proactive when it comes to your taxes.

We have all found ourselves at some point in our lives just continuing to do the same things day in and day out, and we end up falling into that all familiar trap called **"ROUTINE."** This can be good, but it can also be bad. It is funny how conditioned we can become as people (think back to the flea training). Just think about your drive to work, or what you do every morning when you get out of bed, or the way you put on your pants with the same leg first, every time!

On my morning commute to the office I often find myself taking the same roads over and over, and have to remind myself to just "switch it up" in order to break from routine! When I get out of bed in the morning, I find myself doing a few things that are the same every morning. I am positive that if you take the time to notice what you do day to day in your life, you will find the same thing. So, you may be wondering, what point am I trying to make? I am simply suggesting it is easy for all of us to fall into routine, and when we do, especially when it comes to important issues such as how much of our hard-earned dollars should be paid to the government, we can miss opportunities that may exist to retain more of those hard-earned dollars.

Given that we can fall into routine, it is safe to say that professionals can also fall into routine. Over the years of *helping folks secure and grow their retirement wealth, plan their estates, and save significant dollars in taxes,* I have come across a variety of stories that are very compelling. I will share one which I hope will help you make great decisions for your tax future.

One of our clients was getting their taxes done by their CPA whom they had known for a long time. This person was so close to them they were basically a friend of the family. After analyzing their tax structure, we advised them that they could take advantage of significant tax savings if they implemented some of the advanced strategies we knew about. These strategies were all court tested and IRS approved. What was their significant savings? Over $40,000 annually! That's right...over $40,000 more they would keep in their pockets every year! Over a ten year period this would represent roughly $400,000 they would keep instead of giving to the government. Now, the amount of savings for each client is obviously different. We have had clients save much more and much less. Our findings with the clientele we serve, are that typical savings can be around

$30,000 annually! The key for you to take away from this is how important it is to align yourself with someone who is a pro-active tax planner.

Some key questions to ask yourself about your current tax preparer:

1. Has your tax preparer ever proactively shared any new thoughts or ideas over the years?
2. When was the last time your tax preparer brought you a new idea that saved you money in taxes?
3. Are you confident that your tax preparer is doing everything necessary to keep up with changes in the IRS code?
4. When you first met your tax preparer, were you looking for another friend or tax help?

These questions are all very important, and the fourth question is probably the most important. The answer we hear most often on the advanced tax planning side of our firm is, "No, I was not looking for another friend; I was seeking tax advice." This is why a great question/thought in relation to the 4th question above is, "So you were not looking for a friend, but you have created a relationship over time, which is normal. If your situation could be improved and you could save more money each year in taxes, would there be any reason that you wouldn't, NOW, make a change to save that money and keep what is rightfully yours?"

Even though it can be challenging to break relationships, the only logical response is, I am willing to make a change for the better!

We have been working with a variety of different professionals for years and we continually have discussions about how doing a tax reduction plan for someone can really open their eyes to the tax savings available to them. There have been hundreds of thousands of dollars in tax savings that have been uncovered when we have done an in-depth analysis for clients on their tax returns.

This is one huge reason why tax planning is so important. Only a small, select group of professionals in the country actually perform proactive, advanced tax planning. Most tax professionals could, but often find themselves falling into the routine that we mentioned earlier. The American Institute of Certified Tax Coaches has created an opportunity for individuals to gain the training and knowledge needed to go deeper into their taxes and truly look at them in a forward-thinking manner. When tax planning is done on a portfolio, several things are taken into consideration.

First of all, *we are looking at what can be done in the current year to reduce taxation. It is important to note that most of the folks we are able to help with tax planning usually have a significant income and are paying a considerable sum of money in taxes.* The second thing we do is *analyze a client's investment portfolio to create strategies that will reposition their assets, utilizing arbitrage and other means, to create as much tax-free income in the future as possible!*

There is no way to avoid taxes altogether, but if real planning is done, you will keep much more of YOUR money than without planning. The third part of the process is to *adapt continually as new tax laws are created, new loopholes are made, and old laws go off the books or loopholes are closed.* One of the ways we are able to do this is by meeting regularly with our clients to ensure we are up to date on any changes they may have made in their lives.

There are many benefits to tax planning, but the biggest one in my opinion is **to ensure that you are not overpaying the IRS,** by utilizing the very same tax code it created. One of the reasons I became a certified tax coach myself was simply because, as a successful business owner since 2002, it became clear to me that I needed deeper and better strategies to help me legally retain more of my own hard-earned dollars.

As a result, I now have the opportunity to assist many of my clients with some of the same benefits I received from the knowledge gained through the certified tax coach organization. A great way to find an advanced tax planning coach in your area is by visiting the website www.certifiedtaxcoach.com or by sending an email to our helpful team at info@LeanOnTheWall.com. We will do our best to guide you in the right direction!

The key here is to find the right tax coach to assist you with new and innovative planning. As the old saying goes, to keep doing what you are doing but expect different results is insanity!

Your #1 expense in life is TAXES!

Notes:

Michael at a book signing
at Ferrari of Palm Beach

Michael and Samantha supporting one
of their favorite charities, Place of Hope

Left to right: Joel, Samantha, Jael, Justus, Michael & Cyrus

Michael on After the Bell
at Fox Business studios

Michael with Vince Gill
at his home studio

Michael with Sean Hannity at Atlanta studio

Michael at CBS studios in New York

Michael speaking to student body
at Liberty University

Michael and Samantha with Tim Tebow at YMCA Prayer Breakfast

Michael working with the renowned Roger Ibbotson at the NYSE

Michael on Bloomberg

Michael at the New York Stock Exchange

Michael commentating on Fox Business in New York studio

Michael with Brett Baire at the YMCA Prayer Breakfast

Michael and Samantha with Actor Sean Astin at Woodlawn premier

The Michael Wall Show

Michael with Sammy Hagar at his San Fransisco studio

Michael and Cyrus in studio with Paul and Kathy Leone, CEO of The Breakers, Palm Beach

Michael interviewing Chicago at House of Blues

Michael and Samantha in Israel

Michael and Samantha at the entrance to the Tomb of Jesus

Is The Advice You're Getting Right For YOU?

"Wall Street is the only place that people ride to in a Rolls Royce to get advice from those who take the subway" -Warren Buffet

Many consumers find looking for help with their financial affairs to be a challenging task. One reason is simply that many of the firms out there seem to be "all the same" in the eyes of the consumer. Obviously, if everyone looks the same it becomes harder to make a good decision about what is best for your specific situation. You may start to feel helpless. I know how this feels because I am slightly color blind, and sometimes finding the right neck tie to match my outfit can be a challenge! I know this is a silly example, but the helpless feeling can be the same even though the importance of protecting your financial future is much greater.

The reality is a lot of the options that folks have to choose from when it comes to getting financial advice are in many ways the same and look no different to the consumer. This is one of the reasons why the financial world as a whole has gotten such a bad reputation over the years. What started out for the benefit of the consumer has in many ways turned into something that has basically become a financial machine.

You see this played out by the reality that **the level of customer service has gone way down over the years and we keep hearing about lawsuits in which large financial institutions have paid out hefty sums for client neglect or client abuse.**

Understandably, this has caused consumers who really need and want financial help to hesitate instead of actively looking for the right advice.

The reason I felt it necessary to include this chapter in the book was to help folks clearly and simply understand the steps they need to take in order to ensure they are getting the help they need with their financial future. Whether I am working with a client of our firm, coaching a business, or sharing thoughts on different media outlets, I am always sure to mention the fact that not every client is right for us and we are not appropriate for every client.

This can sound a little contradictory, especially when we are still in the process of bringing in new clients. However, it makes a lot of sense if you understand the business model our firm has as well as the financial phases of life that we all go through.

When looking for a financial professional I believe it is just as important to understand their business model (how many clients they want to bring into their firm and what their focus really is), as it is to become familiar with the types of solutions they are prepared to offer. For example, in our firm, we have a specific number of new clients that we are willing to bring into the firm each year, depending on how many advisors we have at the time. This is crucial because I believe service, in many cases, has become a lost art and it is our goal to maintain exceptional service regardless of where our clients are located. As you are searching for a firm this should be a question you ask.

- What is your plan to continue your current level of service and how do intend to improve your service for your clients in the future?

This question will give you some insight into the heartbeat of their firm. Their response to it will also provide clear evidence on whether their focus is just gathering new assets with no real plan to maintain a high level of service, or if they have a clear plan to ensure their clients happiness and success. You definitely want to see results, but I believe that if you are also experiencing a high level of service, it means the professional has insight into your needs and will be able to make better recommendations.

The next important step to ensure you are aligning yourself with the professional who is appropriate for you is to understand the phases of your financial life and which category you land in, as well as which category the advisor you are connecting with lands in.

CAUTION:
When you explore the phases of life and you are currently working with someone who has assisted you with your finances for many years, you will probably find out that that person was probably appropriate to

help you get to where you are today, but may not be appropriate to assist you in navigating your future needs.

Let's uncover the phases of our financial life to better understand who is appropriate.

PHASE 1: Growth and Accumulation

This is the phase we all go through when we are in the working stage of our lives. Often this, phase can include anyone from 18 years of age all the way through 50 years of age. The main focus of this stage is to grow and accumulate assets for the future, and normally there are many years before those monies will be needed for retirement income. Since this is the case, it makes sense to take more risk on the types of investments you select because you have time to recover if the market has a major downturn.

Typically, riskier investments over the long haul will outperform those that are safer in nature. This is the stage when you will often hear from your professional, *"Hang in there! It's going to come back!"* Again, because this stage affords a longer timeframe, waiting for the market to recover and buying while it is low is typically a good choice.

Keep in mind, though, that just because you have more time with this phase, it is still incredibly important to make sure the advice you are receiving will lead you to the best investments. Many investments over a 10 to 20 year span have produced 8% to 12% in returns, sometimes higher.

PHASE 2: Preservation and Distribution

From the very beginning, we can tell that what we are trying to do with our monies in this phase is very different than our goals in the first phase. This phase is often the time when folks are either retired or looking to retire, sometimes called "The Financial Red Zone".

The focus of what we should be trying to do with our wealth at this stage of the game moves toward asset preservation instead of a focus mainly on growth. That is not to say that we do not want to grow our monies in this stage. On the contrary, we certainly do. When we do grow our wealth, however, we need to make sure the total risk is fully understood and look for ways to minimize this risk.

Some questions I like to ask folks in this stage, which happens to be the stage that we specialize in, are…

- What would hurt you more in your retirement future, if you lost 30-40% percent in a year, or made 0% that year on your investments?
- If you could accomplish your goals without taking risk, would you still take risk?
- When you take risk, is it calculated risk?
- What is your primary goal or purpose for your money in the retirement years?

As we listen to the answers to these questions, we come to know the true heartbeat of the client. Often, the clients we work with realize that their monies are there to help them enjoy retirement, but they also want to leave a legacy from what they have worked so hard for that will outlive them. Since our time in this stage is more limited than the first stage, a major loss in our portfolio could significantly affect our retirement, *otherwise known as 20 to 40 years of unemployment.*

The reason why, earlier, I offered the caution about your current advisor is that most often those who specialize do a better job. This is well known in the medical profession for example. Think about it. Let's say you have visited a general practitioner (GP) for many years to get your routine checkups and then one day, through some testing, found out you had a golf ball-size tumor on the right side of your brain. You had a choice as to who would remove the tumor, your GP or a brain surgery specialist. Who would you choose? Most of us would select a specialist for the surgery. It would be unreasonable and unfair to expect the GP that you had visited for routine exams all these years to be comfortable with handling the removal of a brain tumor!

In the same manner, ***it is unreasonable and unfair to expect the financial professional that helped you through your working years to assist you, completely, in the retirement years.*** Not because he or she doesn't want to help, but rather because the challenges of this stage are different, and therefore, the focus and specialty must be different.

This is why we always encourage folks to not only get a second opinion when they are approaching or in retirement, but also be brave enough to make a change even if it means breaking a relationship of some kind. It goes back to the old definition of insanity: to keep doing what you have been doing but expect different results. Another important thought to keep in mind as you ponder this for yourself is...

CRITICAL POINT:

If you don't feel totally comfortable with the current advice you're receiving, then YOU must take steps to reach out for new insight from another source!

Take a few minute's right now to honestly evaluate your current financial advice...

Positives
(Examples: made money, consistent reviews, listens to me, not worried about markets, a plan for taxes, risks, legacy, etc.)

  1)
  2)
  3)

Negatives
(Examples: Never reviews accounts, lost money, concerned about markets, not holistic in nature, etc.)

  1)
  2)
  3)

Only YOU will live out the consequences from your decisions, good or bad, in YOUR future!

53

Notes:

Train Your Brain To See Financial Opportunities

"A pessimist sees the difficulty in every opportunity; an optimist sees the opportunity in every difficulty." – Winston Churchill

D o you remember the old phrase, "What you see is what you get"? It is amazing how this little seven word phrase can affect our lives more than we know. Learning how to see things in the positive can make all of the difference between getting the break we have always wanted and missing it.

Think about it this way, if you are always pondering thoughts like; nothing ever goes my way, or, I am not even going to try because things never work out for me, chances are you are absolutely right! If you didn't think you had a chance from the start, you probably wouldn't even attempt it. This is crucially important, especially when it comes to our finances. The truth is that many people are pretty lazy when it comes to getting ahead in life.

This is why we will probably always have the 99% and 1%. Here's a great quote from Zig Ziglar, "The elevator to the top is always broken. You have to take the stairs." What this means in relation to our finances, is that we may not get it right the first time, but if we keep on looking we will find the answers we need!

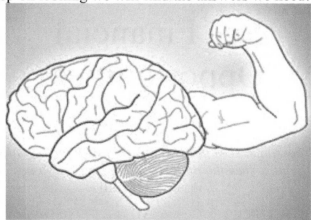

I am a firm believer in the truth that we need to make sure we are hanging around positive people. Have you ever noticed it seems like most of the time people with money hang around other people with money? This is usually because at some level they are intrigued by each other and to some degree, open to learning from each other.

I am always interested in spending time with people that know more and have more than I do. This will ensure that I am always learning and always growing

"Acid destroys the vessel in which it dwells."

If you do your best to avoid negative people in life I can almost GUARANTEE you will be starting down the path of finding some new and fresh ideas which might just be the solutions you are looking for to help you go to the next level. One great way to add positivity to your life is to make the effort to read positive books and listen to encouraging, not just informative, content. There is a lot of "information" out there, but often times it can be shared in a very negative context. You must make a consistent effort to ensure you are getting the information you need relayed to you in a positive manner so you will not be weighed down by negativity!

To start you on that positive journey let me encourage you to subscribe to our radio show, The Michael Wall Show. This can be heard anywhere in the world from any device! To learn more visit, www.LeanOnTheWall.com and click on radio/media.

PAUSE…take a moment to go there now to make sure you start that positive intake!

When you apply this positive thinking to your financial future, it will open some investment doors to you that you didn't notice before. Please note; *I am not suggesting that by doing this you are putting on rose colored glasses and thinking that everything is just perfect.* I am merely implying that when you expect good things to happen they often do. Just as Job said in chapter 3 verse 25, "What I feared has come upon me; what I dreaded has happened to me."

So, just how do we train our brain? First, you want to start by truly believing there are solutions out there that can help you live the retirement you have always wanted, even if you do not know about them yet. Second, thinking this way will give you the freedom to continue on the search of finding the right advisor or investments to get you where you want to go. I know this may sound a little crazy, but trust me, I have been practicing this type of thinking for over 20 years now and it works! I remember that back when I was in college and sold books door to door for several summers, I was taught to brush "Ned Negative" off of my shoulder every morning.

It is important to understand that often we are not naturally positive people. Just think about when you watch the news or read the paper how many actually positive stories you encounter. Or you can just flip on the TV and watch some of the shows which mainly consist of murder, betrayal, downplaying family, kids out of control and many other traits that we would all hope would never happen in our own lives. But that is what many people in the world today feed their minds with on a regular basis. No wonder we live in a negative society. By changing our input and our thought process, it will ultimately change our vision.

Vision Glasses help you see further and see more!

This is why we must make an assertive effort DAILY to combat those negative thoughts by changing our input. I want to encourage you to only focus on positive things for a week and just watch how much better you feel and how many opportunities you see that have always existed, but you had never noticed them before.

How does this help you financially? As I mentioned before, this mindset will give you clarity to take action on investments that are perfect for you. You will be free to do this because you are no longer loaded down by all of the fears and concerns of the world. You will now actually believe, where there is a will there is a way!

It's time to get personal. List below the negative habits you want to eliminate in your life, and positive steps you can take to improve the way you see life. If necessary, come back to this later as more ideas surface. (BE HONEST)

___

Negative Habits to eliminate:

1)

2)

3)

4)

___

Positive steps to take:

1)

2)

3)

4)

Notes:

Ponzi-Proof Your Portfolio

"I went looking for trouble, and I found it." –Charles Ponzi

We hear a lot of talk today pertaining to Ponzi schemes. You may or may not have seen my interview on Fox Business when I discussed with Liz Claman, one of the hosts of "After the Bell," how to protect yourself from a Ponzi scheme, but it is simpler than you might think. If you haven't seen the interview, just Google search "Fox Business" and "Ponzi-proof your portfolio." I believe that it will help bring you further clarity on this issue.

In simple terms, a Ponzi scheme is nothing more than investing your money with someone or some organization that claims your investments are worth a certain value, but you actually own nothing, and they have pocketed the money to pay interest payments to other investors as well as to support their lifestyle. When there are no new monies flowing into the investment, it essentially blows up! This is a very bad thing and certainly something you want to avoid.

· How can I spot a Ponzi Scheme?

In order to spot a Ponzi scheme, you must first know what to look for. Many times, Ponzi schemes are attractive to folks who are interested in being "part of the club." By this I mean there are investors out there who are looking for the ultra-exclusive investment that no one else knows about and almost sounds too good to be true, but they are still excited about the opportunity.

Now, I am not suggesting that there is anything wrong with being exclusive. As you probably know by now from what you have read in this book, we have found at our firm that exclusivity can be a good thing and can sometimes provide the opportunity for better overall service. The point here is simply that if it sounds too good to be true, it might be.

There are some investment styles out there that have earned nice returns every year, year over year, and are perfectly legitimate. My suggestion is to make sure that when you come across something that sounds a little sketchy, make sure you do your homework. Obviously, there have been scams in the past, so we know that the rules that are in place are not foolproof. There is no way to totally be sure that everything will work out as you had planned when you invest, that is why you hear a lot about the idea of taking risk. Any time you have the opportunity to make higher returns you are taking a greater risk and you need to be aware of those risks. Also, make sure you take the time to read offering documents closely and if you are not comfortable with the investment, then don't go through with it. Remember, YOU are the one who ultimately signs your name when you decide to invest somewhere so you need to take the responsibility to do your homework.

  ·   How can I avoid a Ponzi Scheme?

A great way to avoid a Ponzi scheme is to make sure that when you invest your money it is housed with some type of custodian. In simple terms, a custodian is someone who watches over your money (this does not mean they will guarantee your value) to make sure the investments available on their platform are legitimate and legal.

There are several different custodians out there, depending on the type of investment you invest in. For example, if you invest your money in some type of stock, bond, mutual fund, Exchange Traded Fund, option, Real Estate Investment Trust, futures or some other investment, you might see a name like Fidelity, Schwab, Folio, TD Ameritrade or one of many others. I am not suggesting that one is better than the other. These are just organizations that allow monies to be held on a platform where trades can be made.

Normally, these organizations make most of their money when a transaction happens. For example, a stock is bought or sold and they charge a fee for the transaction. They may also charge some other type of annual account fee.

Another type of custodian where your money could be held, even though it works a little differently, is an insurance company. Many investors find it appropriate to invest their money in some type of annuity contract, whether it is a variable, fixed, immediate, or fixed indexed annuity. The investment in this case is sent or transferred to the insurance company, which in turn, creates a contract for the consumer. It is important if you choose one of these investments that you make sure you do your homework to ensure the strength of the company, as they are the ones guaranteeing your money.

Like anything else, there are good and bad for everything.

Annuities can be very confusing and all "sound the same." The reality is they are not all the same, and understanding whether or not they are right for you is important. There is a lot of great information out there on annuities including a study from the Wharton School of Business. Google search "fixed indexed annuities" and "Wharton School of Business study" and you will find a study from professor David F. Babbel discussing the actual returns of some of these products.

Following these steps as well as making the effort to get a referral or two from clients who have already entered into a working relationship with the advisor, will be helpful to avoid this type of situation in your financial future.

Additionally, there are many other types of investments out there that are only suitable for accredited investors. An accredited investor is one that has at least $1,000,000 or more in investable assets. These investments can sometimes be a little tricky to navigate so you want to make sure you do your best to do on-the-ground research, if possible, to ensure the validity of the investment. Some of these investments have benefits you may not be able to find with traditional investments, but you are often taking on a greater degree of risk. Remember, YOU are the one making the final decision to take the necessary steps to invest your money. As the CEO of your portfolio, if you don't feel comfortable with an investment, don't move forward. There is nothing wrong with sitting on the sidelines until you are sure. Just remember, if you sit too long, you may not have the chance to invest in a new opportunity. The key, here, is to find the right balance.

Please remember that not everything and everyone out there is bad, but sometimes investors become so fearful that they don't make any decisions. In those cases, no one wins.

There are probably investments out there you have never heard of that may fit your specific situation and needs. This is why it is crucial to look for the right professional who can help you sort through these decisions. When you take the time, and do the research to find the right professional, you will be enabled to live the type of future you have always wanted. At the same time this will also help reduce worry in your life!

Worry is like a rocking chair. It gives you something to do, but doesn't get you anywhere!

Notes:

Avoiding Financial Amnesia

"I'm involved in the stock market, which is fun and sometimes, very painful." –Regis Philbin

Amnesia: /am'nēZHa/ - (Noun) - A partial or total loss of memory. Now that we know what amnesia is, you're probably asking how in the world this relates to finances! Let me tell you.

We are constantly meeting and speaking with folks at our firm to discuss how we can improve what is currently happening in their portfolio. I am amazed at how many of these folks know what the value of their portfolio was at the end of 2007. But if I ask them what their portfolio value was ten years before that and they are honest about it, most of the time they don't have a clue. In my eyes that is a huge problem.

Most investors know that the markets and many investments go up and down and change in value over time and when you are receiving great advice, your portfolio's value should be going up! It becomes easy, however, for the lazy advisor to share with you how great he or she is doing for you when the market has a great year and yet hope you don't remember what your portfolio value was ten years ago.

We often hold educational events and then meet with potential clients at our office. You would be surprised how many of these folks find out that their portfolio value from several years ago (referring to 2000-2010) is the same or lower than today, without any withdrawals taken to reduce the value!

In my opinion that is simply unacceptable!

Thankfully, this is not always the case, but we see it all too often. The idea of avoiding financial amnesia when it comes to your portfolio is to implement simple, easy-to-follow solutions which will allow you to **make sure you always remember what I call your "Starting Value."** Your starting value is the amount of money you initially invest when first meeting with an advisor. For example; if we work with a new client who decides to invest $5,000,000 with our firm, regardless of any fees or charges, the starting value will always be $5,000,000, unless they invest more monies with us in the future.

Every time we sit down with that client and have a progress meeting to check on their financial status as well as make any changes necessary, we always have a *"Progress Meeting Sheet"* for them. The *"Progress Meeting Sheet"* brings together the three most important portfolio values on one simple form: the client's starting value, their current investment value, and any withdrawals taken out of the portfolio.

This is an easy to understand and helpful tool for our clients because it allows a couple of important things to occur for them.

First, it…

- Gives the client CONFIDENCE he or she will always know what he or she started with.

It gives the client confidence that he or she will always be able to easily see and remember what value they started with, regardless of how many years have passed. The client will know very clearly, even fifteen years from now, what he or she started with on day one. This makes it easy to track how well his or her portfolio is doing.

Second, it...

- Brings ACCOUNTABILITY to the advisor.

This process will bring a strong level of accountability to the advisor. When the advisor knows that every time he or she meets with the client, and the starting value will always be discussed no matter how many years pass, **they know they must perform!**

This is an obvious benefit to the client because it will make it easy for them to know if they need to make a change and find an advisor who is willing, not only to be held accountable to do what is best for the client, but also who is always looking for ways to show them better results!

Following these steps will take a lot of fear, worry, and frustration out of your financial life, which should allow you to enjoy every part of your life even more! Remember, YOU are the only one who can make changes in your future. It is your responsibility to make a change if you are unhappy.

"Yesterday ended last night. Today is a brand-new day and it's yours!"
– Zig Z.

Notes:

Estate Planning That Works

"Death is not the end. There remains the litigation over the estate." –Ambrose Bierce

When it comes to thinking about, discussing, or even starting the process of planning an estate, most individuals shut down or put this planning off. They simply don't want to think about the fact that someday we will all pass away. As Zig Ziglar used to say, "we will be dead a lot longer than we will be alive." I am not trying to depress you. I am just trying to make sure you do what is necessary to have the planning you need in place as soon as possible.

It is an old adage that many people will spend more time planning their vacations than they do planning their lives. Estate planning can be made exciting if we focus our thoughts on the idea of legacy. It is often too easy to get caught up in our day-to-day lives and miss the reality that when we are no longer on this earth and we have arrived at our final, eternal destination, we will have left some type of impact on the world around us.

A couple of questions come to mind when thinking about the impact we make on life after we are gone which can affect many people for years to come.

- What kind of legacy do YOU want to leave?

When you think about legacy, what do you think about? Have you been influenced emotionally, spiritually, or financially by some of your ancestors? What if you were able to leave not only a financial legacy, but also a spiritual and emotional legacy as well? By this I mean how you would impact lives through the organizations or charities you bless financially when you walk out on life. These organizations would then continue on the process of encouraging, uplifting, and challenging people to be the best version of themselves they can be!

Obviously, in order to leave a legacy, you need to have some planning in place so you can maximize your impact. Let's start with the basics. There are three documents you absolutely need to ensure smooth sailing when planning for a basic or smaller estate.

- The first document is a will.

This is not much more than writing down your wishes and to whom you would like your assets to go to when you pass away.

Please note: just because you have a will does not mean you will necessarily avoid probate. Probate is the process of waiting while your estate is settled with the help of attorneys and the courts.

Having a will is one of the beginning building blocks of estate planning.

- The second document is a power of attorney.

This document simply gives authority to someone else to act in the best interest on your behalf when you are unable to make decisions on your own.

- The third document is called a living will. This is simply a document that encompasses a series of questions that you answer to clearly show your wishes and desires if, God forbid, you would need to be kept alive by a life-support system. Having this document in place will definitely make it easier on the loved ones around you.

Once these three initial estate building blocks are in place, you can then move on to more advanced planning if it is necessary. Many times, with the clientele we serve, there is a need for more advanced planning simply because of the size of their portfolios.

Here is another common question that is asked.

- Do I need a trust, and if so, what kind?

In our day-to-day planning with clients we hear this question a lot. Trusts are simply legal arrangements that are set up to protect or carry out more specific directives when it comes to your finances. Many trusts also have the ability to avoid probate.

When it comes to whether or not you need a trust for your estate planning, my first recommendation would be to seek out an estate planning attorney who can further assist you with your specific situation. Since I am not an attorney myself, I simply share with clients some of the options available and then bring in a trusted attorney when these needs arise.

There can be many benefits to having a trust, especially if you have a large estate. One of the most common reasons why investors seek to have a trust set up is to look for ways in which they can legally, morally, and ethically protect their assets from taxes and lawsuits. Many different types of trusts are available to solve a variety of different needs and concerns. In order to decide which type of advanced planning is right for you, a meeting with a professional is a must.

When you finally take the steps to evaluate your investment process as well as to ensure that you are getting all of the help you need on investment, tax, and estate planning, you will be well on your way to **Retire Once and Retire Well!**

Notes:

Notes:

Steward Well

*"Remember the Lord your God. He is
the one who gives you power to be
successful."*
-Deuteronomy 8:18a

I read a book several years back when I was first
starting out in my career that totally changed my
perspective on business, life and wealth. It was
given to me by a great friend whom I truly respected.
Have you ever had someone in your life who you knew
was whole-heartedly interested in nothing more than
the best for you? Well this person was exactly that
kind of friend.

The book he gave me was called *"God Runs My
Business."* This is the story of R.G. LeTourneau, who
was not only a great business man, but also a great man
of God. He had his priorities in line. His inventions
and the impact he made across our nation were
immense. His decision to do a "reverse tithe" and give
90% of all of his wealth and income to God-led
initiatives, while living on only 10%, caused him to
experience radical growth in his business! Doors
opened all over the country for him to share his story.

I am not suggesting the recipe to success is to just give and give and then you will be successful. But when you read scripture it is very clear that if you put God first in your life, He will provide in greater ways than all you can ask or think.

The idea of being a good steward starts in the heart, not the wallet. Have you ever received something from someone who you knew wanted something from you in return? This really cheapens the whole experience of receiving. God is interested in us not only giving to His Kingdom, but also giving our lives as He leads, and doing this with no expectation. Simply doing it because He is worthy and deserving. The best part about following the Creator of all, is that His promises are true. His timing and how He does things may be a mystery at times, but we can fully lean into the fact that if we "seek first His kingdom, all these things will be added unto us" - Matthew 6:33.

Too often we relate success and stewardship to just money, but it is much more than that. It is also how we live our lives, how we treat people, whether or not we love our spouses as Christ loved the church, and much more. All of these things will take effort, but remember ANYTHING worthwhile takes effort.

Stewarding well is a lifelong process and something we will never fully master while on earth. The goal is to continue to "press on towards the mark to receive the heavenly prize" as Paul tells us in Philippians 3:14. I believe one way to improve how we steward our time, talent and treasure is to unplug from the world on a routine basis. Everything today moves at the speed of light. If we never take the time to "unplug" we will always be consumed with the toys, tools and worries of the world. Unplugging requires a physical action to be taken. This would include things like, turning off the TV, shutting your phone down, being intentional about connecting with people who will push you towards the things of God. By doing this you will take back control of your focus and place it where it needs to be, not just on what is in front of you at the moment.

This kind of purpose will keep you from being what Zig Ziglar calls a "wondering generality" in life. You must be willing to do the hard work and not take the easy road. This kind of intentionality will start you down the road to being a good steward.

Another key point in stewarding well is to remember that everything we have or will ever have, even our lives is a gift that can only be obtained by God allowing us to have it. If we can keep this mindset close to our heart, we will realize that everything we have is to be used as a tool for the kingdom.

Here are some helpful questions to help you relate this to your everyday life.

- Do you have a house? Why not think of ways to use your home as a place where you can encourage others and meet the needs of others?
- Do you have a car? When was the last time you gave someone a ride who needed it?
- Have you ever noticed someone that looked as if they could use a boost in their day? Why not give them a twenty-dollar bill and tell them Jesus loves them.

- When was the last time you made an intentional effort to spend time encouraging and listening to someone who needed a listening ear?
- What have you done in the last week to invest in your marriage and children?

I believe if we look at life in this way our days will not be mundane, rather they will be sustained by the blessing of God because our focus is continually on working with Him. After all, Christ was the best example of a steward by giving all He had, His very life, for the forgiveness and cleansing of our sins.

Never forget.

We only get ONE life. Let's steward it well!

Time to change and take action!

Please take a moment, grab a pen and list two or three things that you will strive to change in order to steward your life well. I want to encourage you to **tear this page out** and place it in on your bathroom mirror or somewhere you can see it every day.

Things you are doing well...

1)

2)

Things to implement or change...

1)

2)

Notes:

Make Family A Priority

"You don't choose your family. They are God's gift to you, as you are to them." –Desmond Tutu

I believe peace of mind, contentment and feeling like you belong or have a real purpose, are some of the things that most people desire in their life. There are many things that we can allow to take our time as we go through life. This is why it is extremely important for us to constantly be evaluating what we are allowing to swallow up our time every day.

In our culture today, we have become so self-centered and self-focused, that if most of us are honest with ourselves, we spend little time thinking about, let alone, taking care of the needs of others, especially our families. It can be easy to "take our family for granted," since they are around us all of the time. I believe it is essential to our happiness in life to make an assertive effort to spend quality time with our families. After all, we are raising the next generation.

Don't be so busy building your life that you forget to enjoy life! Take time to <u>STOP</u> and smell the roses.

If you have created a culture in your home where the focus, conversation and lifestyle are all about money, which is temporary and doesn't bring true happiness, I would encourage you to look for ways to spend quality time. Sometimes, it can just be the little things like, taking a hike, or throwing the ball with your kids, taking a walk or many other simple things. This creates an environment allowing the opportunity for meaningful conversation without the distraction of technology always at your fingertips.

One of the techniques I have tried to stick to, even though I fail sometimes, is to put my cell phone away when I come home from the office. With today's technology, there are too many opportunities for distraction; Facebook, Twitter, emails, text messages and many more. None of those things are more important than my wife and children.

I have found that when I stick to this technique several things happen. I have deeper conversations with my family, I am more patient with them and I am more refreshed the next day when I go into the office. I believe this is the case because I have allowed myself to "shut off" mentally the night before. Another thing I have found beneficial, is to take time before going to bed and when I wake up in the morning to read the word of God, otherwise known as the Bible. This allows me to gain perspective on what life is really all about and keep the focus that God really does have a plan for our lives. "For I know the plans I have for you says the Lord…" -Jeremiah 29:11.

One of my favorite quotes from Zig Ziglar says, "Someday we will either say, I am glad I did, or I wish I had." This type of thinking will help us keep the important things in focus.

Over the years of assisting affluent families preserve and grow their wealth, plan their estates, and save in taxes, I have never met with anyone who said they wish they would have spent more time working and less time with their families.

May I encourage you after reading this book to make great decisions financially and take steps to get your entire life in focus; physical, mental, financial, spiritual and family life.

As for my family and I, we wish you success and happiness in your future! I know that "if you do the things you need to do, when you need to do them, the day will come when you can do the things you want to do, when you want to do them!" -Zig Ziglar.

God bless you!

P.S. For more information and insight from Michael, subscribe to the Michael Wall Show on your favorite podcast app.

Notes:

Notes:

Notes:

Books I Highly Recommend

- <u>The Power of Positive Thinking</u> by Norman Vincent Peale
- <u>The Compound Effect</u> by Darren Hardy
- <u>Dare to Dream…Then Do It</u> by John Maxwell
- <u>How to Stay Motivated (Audio book)</u> by Zig Ziglar
- <u>The Total Money Makeover</u> by Dave Ramsey
- <u>God Runs My Business</u> by Albert Lorimer
- <u>The Bible</u> by God
- <u>Think and Grow Rich</u> by Napoleon Hill

"A successful man is one who can lay
a firm foundation with the bricks
others have thrown at him."
-David Brinkley

Contact Information:

To contact Michael and his team for more information about speaking engagements, media appearances, business coaching, or to simply request more information about your retirement issues-

Call: (888) 511-WALL (9255)

Email: info@LeanOnTheWall.com

Visit: www.LeanOnTheWall.com

To buy copies of this book in bulk or to request information about Michael teaching your organization, business or church through the *Retire Well Workbook Series*, call: (888) 511-WALL (9255) or send an email to: info@LeanOnTheWall.com.

Follow the Wall Private Wealth page on Facebook to stay in tune with us, and be sure to subscribe to The Michael Wall Show on your favorite podcast app so you can keep up to date on current financial information.

Wishing you a blessed year!